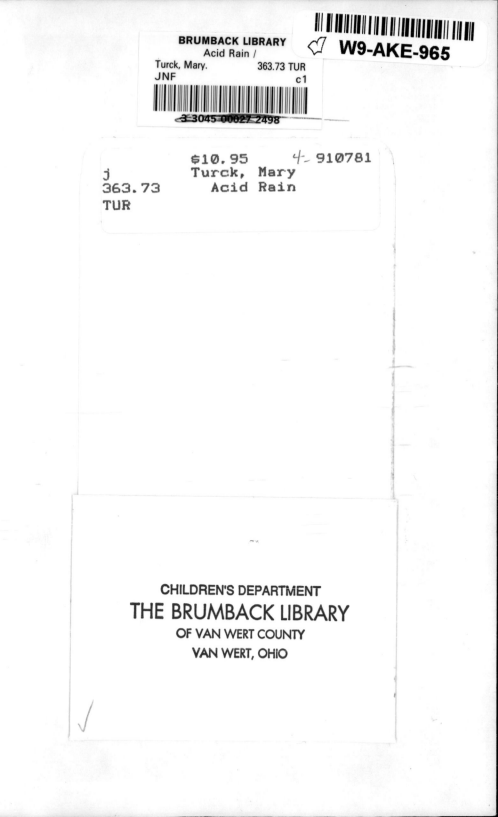

ACID RAIN

BY
MARY TURCK

CRESTWOOD HOUSE

New York

Collier Macmillan Canada
Toronto

Maxwell Macmillan International Publishing Group
New York Oxford Singapore Sydney

Library of Congress Cataloging-in-Publication Data

Turck, Mary.
  Acid Rain / by Mary Turck. — 1st ed.
    p. cm. — (Earth alert)
  Includes bibliographical references.
  Summary: Discusses the sources, destructive effects, and future control of acid rain.
  1. Acid rain—Environmental aspects—Juvenile literature. 2. Acid rain—Environmental aspects—United States—Juvenile literature. [1. Acid rain.] I. Title. II. Series.
TD195.44.T87   1990   363.73'86—dc20   90-35495   CIP
ISBN 0-89686-547-9   AC

Photo Credits

Cover: Peter Arnold, Inc.: (Horst Schafer)
Grant Heilman Photography, Inc.: (Runk/Schoenberger) 4, 11, 13, 29, 36
Earth Scenes: (Michael Habichi) 7; (C.C. Lockwood) 14; (Breck P. Kent) 26; (Doug Wechsler) 30
Journalism Services: (Joseph Jacobson) 8; (John Patsch) 22
Animals Animals: (C.C. Lockwood) 17; (H. Ausloos) 20
Devaney Stock Photos: 25
Superstock: 33
Peter Arnold, Inc.: (Yoram Kahana) 38

CRESTWOOD HOUSE

Macmillan Publishing Company
866 Third Avenue
New York, NY 10022

Collier Macmillan Canada, Inc.
1200 Eglinton Avenue East
Suite 200
Don Mills, Ontario M3C 3N1

Produced by Flying Fish Studio Incorporated

Printed in the United States of America

First Edition

10 9 8 7 6 5 4 3 2 1

CONTENTS

ONE LAKE'S STORY

Muskoka Lake is in Ontario, Canada. It is about one hundred miles north of Toronto. This is a good place to fish, and there are lots of fishing resorts here. But now the people who live in the Muskoka Lake area are worried. Acid rain is changing Muskoka Lake.

The people of Muskoka Lake are watching. After every rain or snowfall, they test lakes and streams. Often they find that a lake is more acid than before the rain. Sometimes they find dead trout floating on the water, too.

Not all rain or snow storms are the same. Those that come from the southwest bring more acid. Much of it comes from the Ohio Valley. Coal-burning power plants and steel mills there help make the acid rain. Winds carry the acid from the United States to Canada. And then it falls into Muskoka Lake, killing fish.

Bright blue, crystal clear . . . and dead—a lake that has been destroyed by acid rain.

A Canadian physicist who lives on the Muskoka River has been watching what has happened to his farm. The water in his well is dark brown. His cauliflower crop doesn't grow well. This scientist is positive that acid rain is to blame.

Much farther north, other scientists are studying the effects of acid. They want to find out exactly what it does to lakes. So they have gone to a lake near Vermilion Bay called Lake 223. This lake is so far north that acid rain doesn't reach it. When the scientists came, it was a pure, clean lake. Then in 1974, they began to put sulfuric acid in the lake. They measured carefully. They wanted to find out what acid does to a clean lake.

The scientists added acid to Lake 223 very slowly. Four years later they saw the freshwater shrimp die out. Fathead minnows stopped reproducing and began to vanish. As Lake 223 became more and more acid, algae mats began to form. Crayfish became sick. After seven years, the lake trout stopped reproducing. All the fish species began to die. So did leeches and mayflies and crawfish.

In 1984, the scientists stopped adding acid. They started to let the lake recover. Slowly some species of fish began to get better. But, the scientists wondered, how long would this recovery take? One scientist says it will take hundreds of years—even if no more acid is added.

Some lakes in Scandinavia and North America are in even worse shape than Lake 223. They have higher acid levels. A very high acid level can kill a lake completely. If the acid rains keep falling, that may happen to Muskoka Lake.

Scientists studied the effects of acid rain by adding sulfuric acid to a lake in Canada and then recording the changes that took place. As time went by,
6   *all the fish species began to die.*

Coal-burning power plants are the main source of acid rain.

THE ACID RAIN CYCLE

The story of acid rain begins with fire. Hundreds of power plants burn millions of tons of coal. Burning coal produces electricity. We all use electricity. We use it for heating and air conditioning. We use it for lights and computers. You can probably name many uses for electric power.

Coal is made of carbon. But coal that is mined is not pure carbon. It has other minerals attached to it. Two of these are sulfur and nitrogen. When coal burns, some of the sulfur is changed to sulfur dioxide. Some of the nitrogen is changed to nitrogen oxides. They escape into the air as poisonous gases. Other chemicals escape into the air through the smokestacks. Among these are mercury, arsenic, and aluminum. Some of these minerals are changed into gases. Others become tiny specks of ash.

Tall smokestacks carry the smoke, ash, and gases high into the air. As the chemicals drift, they may change again. They may react with other chemicals in the air. Sulfur dioxide, for instance, combines with water. This makes sulfuric acid. Nitrogen oxide gas combines with water, too, and becomes another acid. These drops of acid float up into the clouds. But they don't stay up in the air forever.

When the clouds release rain, the acid goes with it. This is acid rain. The acids can come down in snow, too. They can also come down in sleet or fog. Or the acids can come to earth as gases or solids. No matter how they land, acids can cause damage.

Scientists can measure how much acid there is in rain. The measurement is called pH level. The pH scale goes from 0 to 14. A reading lower than 7 on the scale is called acidic. Readings

9

higher than 7 are called basic. Pure water is neutral. It measures 7 on the scale. Normal rain is slightly acid. It has a pH of about 6.5. Rain with a pH of 5.5 is ten times more acid than normal rain. A pH of 4.5 means one hundred times more acid than normal rain. In highly polluted parts of the country, rain with a pH of 4.5 to 5 is common.

ACID RAIN: A SCIENTIFIC DETECTIVE STORY

The time is 1961. The place is Sweden. Once-lively, sparkling lakes are still. Fish no longer leap in the air. All over Sweden, the fish are dying. People are worried. What could be happening to the fish? How can their deaths be stopped?

The Swedish government wanted to find out. So they sent a young scientist named Svante Odén to study the problem.

As Odén worked, he made a surprising discovery. Acid was falling from the sky! This acid was poisoning the lakes and rivers. Odén knew that some small amount of acid was normal in rain. But now he found much more. He showed that the acid in the rain and in lakes had increased greatly since the 1940s.

Odén was not the first person to discover acid rain. A hundred years before him, an English scientist named Robert Angus Smith learned about acid rain.

~ *A pH meter measures the amount of acid present in a sample of rainwater.*

11

In 1872, Smith published the first book on acid rain. He explained that acid rain was caused by burning coal. The burning coal left sulfuric acid in the air. The acid faded colors in cloth and paper. It even caused stones in buildings to crumble.

When Svante Odén took his findings to the newspapers in 1967, they got much more attention than Smith's book. People all over the world read about acid rain. Other scientists began to study acid rain, too.

Today we know that acid rain kills lakes. When a lake is polluted by acid rain, the fish, frogs, and insects in it die. Acid rain also damages trees and crops. Whole forests are being wiped out by the rain.

Acid rain also creates health problems for some people. It hurts their lungs and can make breathing harder. Acid fog can be particularly dangerous to people with asthma or other respiratory problems.

Acid rain corrodes stone in statues and buildings. Famous buildings like the Taj Mahal are being worn away. The United States Capitol building and the Lincoln Memorial in Washington, D.C., have been damaged by acid rain, too.

Higher acid levels are dangerous to drinking water, as well. Some water pipes are made from lead or copper. Acid can dissolve these metals. Then some copper or lead ends up in the water we drink. These metals don't make a person ill right away. But over time they can cause serious damage.

Acid rain is a bigger problem today than when it was first discovered. More lakes and forests are in danger. More of the water we drink and the air we breathe is threatened.

Acid rain destroys not only lakes and forests. The pockmarks on the U.S. Capitol show how the rain has eaten away at a national landmark.

Sulfur plants like this one in Louisiana release large amounts of sulfur dioxide, which turns into sulfuric acid, the main ingredient in acid rain.

SOURCES OF ACID RAIN

Many people blame the electric power companies for acid rain. Some companies say that is unfair. They claim that acid rain comes from many sources, even trees and flowers. What is the truth?

Pure water has a pH of 7, which is exactly neutral. Normal rain is not quite pure water. It has small amounts of acids, which come from nature. But acid rain has much more acid in it, especially sulfuric acid. About 95 percent of the sulfur dioxide in the air is made by humans. Electric companies produce 71 percent of this acid. Most of this comes from power plants that burn coal.

In the United States, electric power plants are the biggest source of sulfur dioxide. In Canada, metal smelters make most of the sulfur dioxide. These metal smelters also burn coal.

Other sources of sulfur dioxide are homes that are heated by coal and by industries that burn it. Fuels other than coal can make sulfur dioxide, too.

Some of the nitric acid in acid rain does come from nature. Nitric acid is made from nitrogen oxides. And some nitrogen oxides are produced by forest fires. But 90 percent of it comes from human sources. Power plants are also a major source of nitrogen oxides. Home and industrial boilers make some, too. So do cars, trains, and planes.

The United States makes more nitrogen oxides than any other country in the world. It also makes more sulfur dioxide. Every year Americans send about 33 million tons of sulfur dioxide into the air. Canadians send another 5.5 million. Europeans send 55 million tons. The rest of the world contributes about 16.5 million tons each year.

Countries that make acid rain do not always get it back, however. Once smokestacks send pollution high into the air, winds can carry it for hundreds of miles. So one state or country can send acids far away.

EATING THE FISH

Fish can still live in a lake with a low acid level. They just get ill or they don't grow. Sometimes they fail to reproduce. But when the acid levels get high enough, all the fish die.

Acids also leach metals from the bottom of the lake. The mud in every lake contains metals. They are not dangerous as long as they stay in the mud and rocks. But the acid draws them out. It dissolves them in the water. This is what leaching means. Once the metals get in the water, they can kill fish.

Aluminum is one of these metals. When acid frees the aluminum, the fish "breathe" it in. The metal coats and burns their gills. Mercury is another of these metals. Fish in acid lakes have more mercury in their bodies than fish usually contain. And scientists say this metal is dangerous to humans. The government has told people to limit the amount of fish they eat from some lakes and rivers. Sometimes it warns people not to eat any fish from certain lakes. Children and pregnant women are in the most danger from mercury.

When the acid level in a lake becomes too high, fish and all other life forms eventually die.

17

Acid rain creates two other problems for fish. First, it can harm or kill a whole generation of young fish. Acid rain often hits lakes in the spring, when fish are laying eggs. Because eggs and young fish are weaker than fully grown ones, spring acid rain can do a lot of harm.

The second problem is that acid rain can kill off much of the fishes' food supply. As a lake becomes more acid, other animal species die off. Leopard frogs, northern pike, toads, and spring peepers disappear. Finally, the lake may be completely poisoned by acid. Then it looks beautiful, blue, clear—and empty.

Different kinds of fish can live with different amounts of acid. Northern pike live longer than trout or salmon. In the end, though, all fish are in danger. The acid in the lakes affects the fish, flies, clams, frogs, and other lake life. But that is not all. Ducks and geese and loons all depend on lakes for their food. When lakes and fish are poisoned or die, the birds suffer, too.

That is what scientists found happening in New York State. In the late 1970s, a biologist was sent to survey lakes in the Adirondack Mountains. He quickly found 212 very sick lakes. His study showed very bad news for lakes in the Adirondacks. Out of every four lakes, one is too acid for fish to live in it. Another is threatened.

TREES AND CROPS

Scientists have studied acid rain for a long time now. They have found widespread acid rain damage to trees and forests. The effect acid rain has on crops is not as clear. Scientists are sure that there is some damage to crops from acid rain. But they need further studies.

The damage to trees was particularly clear on Camels Hump Mountain in Vermont's Green Mountains. In 1965, the peak, which is 4,100 feet high, was covered with fragrant evergreen forests. Some of the red spruce on the highest slopes were three hundred years old. But by 1983, almost half the red spruce on the highest slopes were dead. Some stood like tall skeletons, while others had been blown over by winter winds.

Nor was the killing limited to the mountain's top. At the base of Camels Hump, almost one of every four sugar maples had died. According to scientists, the cause is acid rain. And the damage is not confined to Vermont. Forests all across the eastern United States and Europe are dying because of acid rain and fog.

Acid rain is hardest on trees high up on a mountain, which is often shrouded in mist or fog. So the trees spend much of their time bathed in acid. But trees also suffer because of changes in the soil. Acid rains leach metals from the soil. Then trees "drink" the metals as their roots take up water.

Scientists have found that trees on Camels Hump have three times as much aluminum as they did 25 years ago. Scientists don't know exactly how aluminum hurts trees or how acid rain weakens and kills trees. But they do know that trees are dying in areas that get a lot of acid rain.

Scientists do not yet have enough information on the effects of acid rain on crops. Some scientists who work for power companies claim that acid rain is good for crops. They say it puts nitrogen and sulfur in the soil, and this, they claim, helps to feed the crops.

Other scientists say this idea is just plain crazy. They point out that soil types vary greatly. Some soils are naturally more acid than others. Different soils need different kinds of fertilizers, and so do different kinds of crops. So it is hard to tell exactly what effect acid rain will have on farm crops. Many farmers regularly test their soil. Then they add what is needed to bring it back in balance. In Sweden, the Ministry of Agriculture says acid rain has changed the soil. There farmers have to put more lime on their fields because of the acid rain.

Acid soils can kill useful insects and bacteria. Bacteria are needed for the growth of certain plants. Many kinds of worms work for the health of the soil in many different ways. The worms can't live with high acid levels either.

Then there are the metal problems. Acid rain dissolves metals in the soil. Like spruce trees, grasses and other plants "drink" metals along with water, They are then eaten by cows and other farm animals. So far scientists have not found dangerous levels of mercury in these animals. They have found high mercury levels in seals, ducks, and fish in the far north, however.

AN ANGRY NEIGHBOR

"Do you continue to call people who dump garbage over your fence friends?" That question was asked by an angry member of Canada's Parliament.

Canada suffers more from acid rain than the United States does, and much of it comes from the United States. This rain poisons Canada's lakes. It has killed 14,000 of them. At least 13

Acid rain dissolves metals in the soil. When animals eat the grass in these areas, they can become ill.

rivers in Canada are "acid dead." Maple syrup farmers in Quebec say acid rain is killing their trees as well.

Acid rain costs Canadians hundreds of millions of dollars every year. So the country has passed laws to force its electrical companies to cut down on pollution. But Canada can't stop U.S. power plants from sending acid in its direction.

U.S. power plants send tons of acid to Canada. The Gavin power plant is a good example. Every hour each of its boilers burns 600 tons of coal. Its 1,103-foot-tall smokestack sends gases high into the air and across the border into Canada. (The higher the smokestack, the farther the gases can go.)

Gavin is not the only polluter. Hundreds of power plants are spread across the United States and Canada. Sixty of the largest plants are in the Ohio Valley, within easy reach of Canada.

Canada has tried to get the U.S. government to prevent the pollution. But so far, U.S. presidents have asked for more studies instead, making the Canadians very angry.

Canadians feel that the United States doesn't care about their problems. They point to U.S. politicians who still claim that acid rain is a "minor" problem. As long as the United States keeps "dumping its garbage over the fence" into Canada, these neighbors will have problems being friends.

Much of the acid rain damage in Canada is caused by pollution from U.S. power plants.

U.S. HOT SPOTS

Acid rain does not fall evenly across the country or the world. It is concentrated in certain areas.

As we have seen, Canada gets heavy doses of acid rain. So does the northeastern United States. As early as the 1960s, scientists from Cornell University tested rain and snow in New Hampshire. They found high acid levels there.

States in the Northwest also get acid rain. John Harte, a scientist at the University of California at Berkeley, studies the western side of the Rocky Mountains in Colorado. Harte says that "over and over again" rain and snow show very high acid levels. This pollution probably comes from Los Angeles, not from the east.

Minnesota is also concerned about acid rain. As Minnesota Congressman Gerry Sikorski explains, people there have a special reason to be worried: "We're the Land of Ten Thousand Lakes. Tourism is our third-largest industry and produces over 200,000 permanent, full-time jobs." What's more, Sikorski says, residents love to fish. "On opening day in May, one out of every three Minnesotans is on lakes, fishing. It's part of our lives."

Minnesota is also concerned about Canadian power plants. In 1977, Canada planned a coal-burning power plant at Atikokan, Ontario. That's just 35 miles from the Minnesota border and close to the Boundary Waters Canoe Area. So Minnesota officials, worried about nearby lakes and forests, challenged Canada's plans. Canada angrily replied: "Minnesota has 22 coal-burning plants which send acid rain in our direction."

Acid rain threatens some of our simplest pleasures—a leisurely day spent fishing on a beautiful lake.

Since then, both sides have learned a lot. They know that the United States sends far more acid rain to Canada than it gets back. And Minnesota has taken big steps to stop producing acid rain. Many people say that its laws are the strictest acid rain controls in all of North America.

Since altitude also plays a part in the acid rain drama, lakes high in the mountains are hardest hit. Trees on tall mountains die first. So mountain ranges like the Adirondacks in New York and the Rockies suffer a lot from acid rain. But they are not alone. More than half of the United States is affected by acid rain. The problem stretches from this country across the globe.

A GLOBAL PROBLEM

"Forest death" is an epidemic in Europe. Germany's famous Black Forest has been hit especially hard by this disease. It is losing trees at an alarming rate. One study showed more than a million acres of trees affected by acid rain. Fir trees died first. Then the spruce and the pine trees went. Later studies found that more than half of the forests in Germany are affected. Nor is the problem limited to Germany. In a nearby country, more than 300,000 acres of trees have been killed.

In Africa and South America, fires set by people in forests and grasslands are a major problem. The smoke sends a haze over wide areas, filling the air with acid fog and mist and rain. The fires also pollute the air with other chemicals. One scientist says that the air

Acid rain takes its toll on a forest.

is "like soup cooking." Fires, of course, destroy some of the forests. But more plants and trees are killed by pollution.

Even the Arctic Circle is beginning to feel acid rain. Acid rain, like other kinds of air pollution, circles the entire globe.

Trees and plants are not the only things destroyed by acid rain and pollution. Not even stones are safe! The Parthenon, a marble temple that has stood for centuries in Greece, is now dissolving. Saint Paul's Cathedral in London is also being destroyed. In West Germany at Herten Castle, a statue has stood since 1702. A 1908 photograph of the statue shows a beautiful woman in flowing robes. By 1969, the statue looked like a blob. Acid in the air had destroyed a work of art.

Buildings and art in the United States suffer, too. One government study done in 1979 showed that, even then, acid damage to property cost more than $2 billion each year. That damage is getting worse. Another study in 1985 showed property damage each year of more than $5 billion.

CONTROLLING ACID RAIN

There are ways to control acid rain. One way is to cut down on the amount of sulfur dioxide we put in the air. Another is to cut down on the amount of nitrogen oxides we put in the air. That means putting limits on coal-burning plants. It also means limits on cars and trucks.

Fine works of sculpture are slowly being destroyed by acid rain.

Some factories have added scrubbers to their smokestacks. These capture dangerous sulfur gases from the smoke before they reach the air.

There are five ways to reduce these gases from power plants. Energy conservation is the first and best way. A second way is to burn low-sulfur coal in power plants. Cleaning the coal by smokestack scrubbers as it burns can help. Cleaning the coal before it is burned is a fourth approach. Finding alternate sources of energy is also a solution. None of these ways is magic. None alone is the answer.

Energy conservation is a key approach. If we use less electricity, the power plants will produce less. That means burning less coal. Burning less coal means less acid in the air.

Conservation is mostly voluntary. If people make an effort to use less energy, then it can work. People can save energy by keeping the heat turned down and cooling systems off. They can choose to live with cooler homes in the winter and warmer offices in the summer. They can use fewer electric appliances. Do you think people are willing to save energy?

Burning low-sulfur coal is a second step. High-sulfur coal gives off more sulfur when it burns. That means more acid in the air. Low-sulfur coal gives off less sulfur when it burns. This cuts down on sulfur dioxide emissions. It does not stop them completely.

Using low-sulfur coal costs more, however. This would raise the price of electricity. Thousands of people work at mining high-sulfur coal. They would lose their jobs. So people have to ask if cutting down on acid in the air is worth the price. Who should pay these costs?

Then there are smokestack scrubbers. Scrubbers capture some of the sulfur from smoke. They get it before it reaches the air. The captured sulfur is combined with other things, like lime. This makes a semiliquid mess that looks like wet cement. This can be a problem, too. Where should the captured sulfur go? One power plant captures 4,000 tons of the sulfur mixture every day!

A federal law says that all new coal-burning plants must now have scrubbers. But there are still many old plants without scrubbers.

Some plants are already trying the fourth plan—cleaning the coal before it is burned. This also helps to reduce sulfur emissions. But this kind of cleaning does not work very well.

Finally, there is the search for alternate energy sources. One alternate source is nuclear power. But many people think nuclear power may create problems even worse than acid rain. Another source is power from the sun—solar power. And there is wind power. These two sources have hardly been tried.

There's also the problem of nitrogen oxides produced by cars and trucks. How can we cut down on pollution from cars and trucks? First, more fuel-efficient cars would burn less gasoline. Second, cars could be designed to burn more cleanly. Scrubbers could be put on the cars' exhaust systems.

Of course, driving less would also mean less pollution. People could ride bicycles and buses instead of driving. Car pools mean fewer cars on the road. Good public transportation makes it easier to drive less. Driving less and fighting pollution take a lot of individual effort.

Power companies won't make these changes on their own. Neither will carmakers. To get action, the government must make laws. The government can order antipollution steps. Some states already have strong emission-control laws. Some of these laws

These high-tech windmills are one alternative to coal-burning power plants.
They use the wind to produce electricity.

limit the amount of pollution from power plants. Others apply to factories or cars.

One state or country can't stop acid rain. Even if Minnesota has good laws, acid rain will still come from other states. Even if Canada has strict laws, it will still get acid rain from the United States. Acid rain is a worldwide problem. The solution must come from many countries.

Still, there is a lot that one country can do. The United States produces much of the sulfur dioxide and nitrogen oxides in the world. If we passed strict emission-control laws in this country, we would help reduce acid rain throughout the world.

THE FUTURE

Acid rain kills trees and lakes. It kills fish and flies and clams. It kills people, too. In 1982, the U.S. Congress Office of Technology Assessment studied acid rain in the United States and Canada. People there found that sulfur pollution kills about 51,000 people each year. As many as 250,000 people get sick from this pollution. These people may be ill with lung disease or heart disease. Or they may have other infections that are made worse by the pollution.

Acid rain doesn't kill quickly, like a bullet to the head. Instead, the sulfur chokes its victims slowly. Pollution turns the air to poison. In many cities, the poison stays for days at a time. People's eyes burn and their throats feel raw. Some find it difficult to breathe, especially people with asthma. Pollution is particularly dangerous for older people and those with heart or lung conditions, or even the flu. Pollution can kill them.

Acid rain will not go away by itself. We need to take action to stop it. Unless the world's governments and people do something to end it, the problem will remain.

The power companies and carmakers are well organized. They say that acid rain is not such a serious problem. Or that it needs more study. Or that emission controls are too expensive. And while they talk, the rain keeps falling.

BLOCKING ACID RAIN CONTROLS

Our government can't stop rain from falling. But it can pass laws to cut down on sulfur dioxide emissions. If the sulfur doesn't go into the air, then it can't make acid there.

In the 1980s, the president did not approve any new laws about acid rain. At first, President Reagan said the destruction of trees was responsible for air pollution. Then he said more study was needed. When government experts proved acid rain was a problem, he still didn't act.

Canadians believe that he just didn't want to cooperate. They tried to cut sulfur dioxide emissions. In 1982, Canada proposed to

cut the amount of these emissions in half in both countries. The United States said no.

In 1984, there was a big meeting in Canada. Countries from Europe and North America met to talk about acid rain. Many of them agreed to cut down on sulfur dioxide emissions. The United States refused to sign the agreement.

Early in 1990, Congress and President George Bush proposed some new laws to stop acid rain. Critics say their plans do not go far enough in stopping acid rain. They are especially angry that the plans still allow power plants to burn high-sulfur coal.

The power companies and carmakers do not want stricter laws. The scientists they hire argue that pollution is not such a serious problem. They take out ads in newspapers to influence what we think. All of these efforts have helped to stop or delay antipollution laws.

For industry, the bottom line is what a cleanup will do to its profits. Environmentalists point out that acid rain costs billions. But industry, they say, doesn't pay the bill. The power companies don't pay for dead fish. The carmakers don't pay doctor bills for people with asthma. The coal industry doesn't pay for dead maple trees. It doesn't pay for dying lakes and corroded statues. It doesn't pay for burning eyes and aching lungs.

As more and more people learn about acid rain, the pressure for change grows. Scientists around the world are pushing for changes. They want strict controls on sulfur dioxide emissions. They also want energy conservation.

As scientists learn more about acid rain, they can develop new ways of preventing it.

IN MEMORY OF
MAN

2,000,000 B.C. — A.D. 2030

HE WHO ONCE DOMINATED
THE EARTH —

DESTROYED IT

WITH HIS WASTES,
HIS POISONS, AND
HIS OWN NUMBERS.

WHAT YOU CAN DO

Sometimes hearing about problems like acid rain is discouraging. You may begin to feel hopeless. You may think: "What can I do? I'm just one person. This is an awfully big problem."

The first step in stopping acid rain is learning about it. Now you have read one book. You will probably see more stories about acid rain on television or hear about it on the radio. Newspapers will also run stories about acid rain. You can learn a lot from all of them. But keep in mind that many of them will quote "experts." Sometimes one "expert" will contradict another. How can you tell who is right?

One thing to look for is who is paying the expert. For example, a senator from a state with lots of high-sulfur coal mines may speak. He or she is likely to downplay acid rain problems because the mines create a lot of jobs for voters in the state. The senator may be warned that acid rain laws will hurt their business.

The Electric Power Research Institute may be quoted too. It is funded by power companies. So it may say, for business reasons, too, that acid rain is not a serious problem. Many independent scientists say something different. They often say that acid rain is a large and dangerous problem.

There is another way to figure out whom to believe. That is to compare the evidence. For example, one recent study said that the acid rain problem is getting better. This study used computer models. According to these theoretical models, only a few New York lakes are hurt by acid rain. But in another study, described earlier in this book, scientists actually tested one thousand New York lakes. They found much greater damage to the lakes.

A tombstone in Hawaii suggests what could happen if people do not begin to take care of the environment.

You can learn more about acid rain by writing for more information to concerned groups. Some of these groups are listed in this book in the section called "For More Information."

You can also find information close to home. To do this, you can contact local groups. Some of them know about acid rain and other water problems. If you live in a city, you could write or call your local water treatment plant. If you live in the country, you might want to contact your county extension office. Find out what they know about acid rain. Ask what other water problems exist in your area.

You can also work to educate other people. Maybe you belong to a 4-H club or Girl Scout or Boy Scout group. Your group could schedule a program about acid rain. Your science class could make this a special study project. You might want to study ways of energy conservation. You could also find out about alternative energy sources.

Finally, you can write to people in government and ask their help. Acid rain is a problem too big for just one person. They are working on it, too. Tell them about your interest in acid rain. Ask what they are doing to solve the problem. Tell them what you think needs to be done. You can write to your representative in Congress, your senator, or even the president. You can also write to your state legislators, city council, mayor, or governor.

Acid rain is a danger that human beings created. Now we need to work together to stop it.

FOR MORE INFORMATION

For more information about acid rain, write to:

Acid Rain Information Clearinghouse
  Center for Environmental Information, Inc.
33 S. Washington Street
Rochester, NY 14608

The Environmental Defense Fund
1616 P Street NW
Washington, DC 20036

Interagency Task Force on Acid Precipitation
722 Jackson Place NW
Washington, DC 20006

National Audubon Society
801 Pennsylvania Avenue SE
Washington, DC 20003

National Clean Air Coalition
1400 16th Street NW
Washington, DC 20036

National Wildlife Federation
1400 16th Street NW
Washington, DC 20036

Sierra Club
408 C Street NE
Washington, DC 20002

U.S. Environmental Protection Agency
401 M Street SW
Washington, DC 20460

FOR FURTHER READING

Gay, Kathlyn. *Acid Rain*. New York: Franklin Watts, 1983.

————. *Ozone.* New York: Franklin Watts, 1990.

Miller, Christina, and Louise Berry. *Acid Rain: A Source Book for Young People.* New York: Simon & Schuster, 1986.

Pringle, Laurence. *Rain of Troubles*. New York: Macmillan, 1988.

GLOSSARY

acid *A substance with a pH lower than 7; for example, vinegar.*

acid rain *Rain that contains higher than normal amounts of acid.*

altitude *Height above sea level.*

base *A substance with a pH higher than 7; for example, ammonia.*

corrosion *Process of being worn or eaten away.*

emission control *Cutting down on the amount or kind of polluting gases given off by an industrial plant or motor vehicle.*

high-sulfur coal *Coal with 3 percent or more sulfur content.*

leach *To dissolve chemicals and carry them away from their source.*

low-sulfur coal *Coal with less than 1 percent sulfur content.*

nitric acid *An acid made up of nitrogen, hydrogen, and oxygen* (HNO_3).

nitrogen oxides *Molecules made up of nitrogen and oxygen.*

pH scale *Scale used to measure how acid or how base a substance is.*

pollutant *Any one of a number of substances that make the air or water impure or dirty.*

scrubbers *Devices that remove sulfur from the gases given off by burning coal.*

smelter *A very hot furnace used to refine metals.*

sulfur dioxide *A molecule made up of one atom of sulfur and two atoms of oxygen (SO_2).*

sulfuric acid *The acid formed by hydrogen, sulfur, and oxygen (H_2SO_4).*

INDEX